WHERE'S THE PASSION FOR EXCELLENCE IN THE CHURCH?

Shaping Discipleship Through Ministry and Theological Education

Carnegie Samuel Calian

MOREHOUSE PUBLISHING
WILTON, CONNECTICUT

Morehouse Publishing
78 Danbury Road
Wilton, Connecticut 06897

Library of Congress Cataloging-in-Publication Data

Calian, Carnegie Samuel.
  Where's the passion for excellence in the church?: shaping discipleship through ministry and theological education / by Carnegie Samuel Calian.
      p.   cm.
    Bibliography: p.
    ISBN: 0-8192-1500-7
    1. Theology—Study and teaching—United States. 2. Theological semi-naries—United States. 3. Church renewal—United States.
  I. Title.

BV4030.C35   1989   89-33516
207'.73—dc20   CIP

Printed in the United States of America
          by BSC LITHO
          Harrisburg, PA

To
The Pittsburgh Theological
Seminary Community
and the graduates
who have added an
exciting dimension to my life and ministry

Other Books by Carnegie Samuel Calian

Today's Pastor in Tomorrow's World (revised edition)

The Significance of Eschatology in the Thoughts of Nicolas Berdyaev

Berdyaev's Philosophy of Hope (revised edition)

Icon and Pulpit: The Protestant-Orthodox Encounter

Grace, Guts and Goods: How to Stay Christian in an Affluent Society

The Gospel According to the Wall Street Journal

For All Your Seasons: Biblical Directions through Life's Passages

Contributing Author

The New Man: Orthodox-Reformed Dialogue

Byzantine Fellowship Lectures

Encyclopedia Britannica (15th edition)

The Encyclopedia of Religion, edited by Mircea Eliade

Contents

Preface vii

Acknowledgments ix

Chapter 1.
Where's the Passion for Excellence in the Church? 1

Chapter 2.
Is the Local Church a Seminary? 7

Chapter 3.
The Challenge of John 3:16 for Church and Seminary . . . 17

Chapter 4.
Toward a Common Curriculum for Parish and Classroom . 25

Chapter 5.
Beyond Burnout: The Journey to Renewal 33

Chapter 6.
Characteristics of Excellence in Clergy Leadership 41

Chapter 7.
Marketing the Church's Ministry 45

Chapter 8.
What Can Churches Expect from Seminaries? 51

Postscript 57

Bibliography 59

Preface

Mainline churches today are seeking a reversal of the past decades of decline in membership and loss of influence in society. The situation is serious. Most of us know there is no easy panacea to the problem. The modest task within these pages is to suggest how pastors and educators working together can contribute to a new vitality among mainline churches. The demand for excellence calls for constant improvement and openness to change.

This volume seeks to stimulate reflection on the needed steps to achieve an attitude of excellence in the context of change among our churches and seminaries. Attaining this goal requires greater integration between the current practice of ministry and theological education.

Unfortunately, there is not sufficient communication today between churches and seminaries. Mutual influence and education are needed to produce more excellent witnesses for the sake of Christ.

There is no single definition of excellence; generally it will be understood to mean that quality of church life that offers a caring attitude communicated through competence, an innovative spirit, and enthusiasm. Excellence is a goal for which we strive; it is a process rather than a final status. Churches and seminaries with a passion for excellence can lead the People of God (clergy and laity) to enhance their discipleship in society.

This educating process calls for endless coordinating between the realities of parish life and the curriculum taught in the seminary classroom. This integration calls for constant engagement and reflection to build trust and produce excellence.

The present minimal contacts between churches and theological schools make this an enormous challenge for both parties. Unless we are mutually motivated with a passion for excellence, neither the church nor the theological school will realize their common expectations, namely, to nurture believers into maturity for the kingdom's sake. The following pages seek to provide insights and suggestions to move us forward into renewal and excellence in discipleship.

Acknowledgments

Grateful acknowledgment for this volume goes to Pittsburgh Theological Seminary—faculty, staff, students, directors and graduates. The seminary has been a learning laboratory where I have reflected on the aspects of renewal needed in ministry and theological education today.

I wish also to express thanks to the following publications: *The Christian Century, Christian Ministry, TSF Bulletin, Presbyterian Outlook,* and *Panorama.* The pages of those journals have aided me at different stages of my thinking and have given me an opportunity to express myself. Writing and teaching have always been important to me and my position at the seminary has enabled me to engage in the more difficult task of implementing in part what has been written and taught.

My list of acknowledgments would be incomplete without heartfelt thanks to Linda Smith, my secretary, for her patience and perseverance in typing the manuscript and to my marriage partner and copy editor of thirty years, Doris Zobian Calian, who has enriched my life.

Of course, I take responsibility for the content of this study. Hopefully, these pages will be useful in furthering and enhancing a stewardship of excellence and enthusiasm for the church's mission in our local and global neighborhoods. Special thanks to E. Allen Kelley, Publisher at Morehouse for approaching me with the idea of a book on this theme.

Carnegie Samuel Calian
Pittsburgh Theological Seminary

Chapter 1.

Where's the Passion for Excellence in the Church?

Unfortunately today, "Made in U.S.A." does not necessarily mean the first choice in the marketplace. There is a growing clamor at home and abroad for excellence. Does this passion for excellence prevail in our churches?

Thomas J. Peters coauthored with Nancy Austin another bestselling book, entitled *A Passion for Excellence,* in which the qualities of excellence are reduced to three essential factors: *First,* take exceptional care of your customers via superior service and superior quality; *second,* constantly innovate; and *third,* listen, trust, and respect the dignity and creative potential of each person in the organization.

In short, excellence is built on a *caring attitude,* a quality we hope also exists in church and seminary communities, but something we can never take for granted. We have to work on this caring attitude toward one another all the time. Next, *innovate constantly;* translated into the church's jargon it directs us to the prophetic task of challenging the status quo continually. Finally, excellent organizations have *turned-on people*—where everyone has worth. This is a basic lesson that the church also teaches. Everyone has ownership in the enterprise as we work toward the welfare of all.

Is there a sustained effort for excellence in the church, based upon this threefold standard—(1) a caring attitude, (2) an innovative spirit, and (3) committed (turned-on) people? Probably not, and the fault lies with us—clergy as well as laity.

Are We in a State of Mediocrity?

Many of us have discovered through bitter experience and disappointment that not all members of the "helping professions" are excellent. We are aware of the mounting number

1

of malpractice suits confronting doctors and lawyers. Even the clergy are no longer exempt from the pitfalls of malpractice.

Currently, in the field of law, attorneys grade each other. The results are printed in the *Martindale-Hubbell Directory* and widely circulated within the profession. The grading format is *A, B, C,* and *V.* Attorneys must first ascertain if the lawyer being evaluated is sufficiently honest in his or her practice. If so, that person receives a *V* and is then eligible for entry in the directory. The evaluator then proceeds to determine if the person ought to be in category *A, B,* or *C.* The majority of attorneys receive a *B* grade with the remainder split among the *A* and *C* categories. This list is published annually, and the attorney's standing is subject to annual review. The qualities sought in the evaluating process are as follows: (1) competency in understanding the law and client's needs; (2) conscious practice of one's ethics and adherence to the ethical code of the profession; and (3) a meaningful level of trust between the attorney and clients as well as colleagues.

Can you imagine what it would be like to have pastors grade one another for a directory? For instance, are pastors of larger churches more excellent than pastors of smaller churches? Such a generalization would be absurd! Yet, in discussions with a number of pastor-seeking committees, I find the church's size is a factor in the committee's assessment of the "quality" of the pastor they seek to call.

And for that matter, what criteria would we develop for grading and evaluating congregations? Is there an unspoken consensus among us that congregations simply do not live up to their potential, receiving low to mediocre marks in discipleship and commitment? How often has it been your observation that churches of whatever size have only a small circle of committed workers? The majority of the membership are observers. Or for instance, take the actual membership roll and ask how accurate are the statistics. Do you remember the last time your church trimmed its membership roll? Often the officers of the church are hesitant to act in this matter, lest they offend someone. Our membership standards in practice often do not measure up to requirements found in many service clubs in our neighborhoods.

Where is the passion for excellence that calls for discipline in the church?

Turning to our seminaries, we find that grade time at the end of every term is a period of stress for students and faculties. In all honesty, we are really not sure we are measuring what needs to be measured. Is there any significant correlation between performance in ministry and grades achieved? By the same token, student evaluations of faculty often do not measure what is taught or has transpired in class. For some faculty, student evaluations are real irritants; there are faculty who no longer wish to be graded in life. Do the churches and seminaries truly want excellence in their professional servants?

If we surmise that the church is not really interested in excellence, ought we then to be more accepting of less, including our declining membership? It is not my intention to be pessimistic, but realistic in regard to our present position in society.

There are those who strongly feel that we are in a general state of mediocrity. Surely, we would all agree that there is much to improve. Why are churches losing status in society? What ought to be done to increase interest and commitment? Gallup, in a recent survey, asked people what churches can do to increase the interest of the public in religion. The response fell into six categories:

1. *Select ministers who are most intelligent.* (If our goal is a learned clergy, intelligence certainly ought to be a factor among those called to serve.)
2. *Arrange more social activities around the church.* (Are activities sufficiently inclusive and adequately prepared?)
3. *Become more modern and liberal.* (I found this response surprising given the rebirth of conservatism and fundamentalism in recent years. Perhaps today's church dropouts are still reacting to the legalism connected with restrictive churches. Being a member of a church fellowship ought to be joyous and fun as well as work.)
4. *Eliminate hypocrisy.* (We know that the true "saints" of the church are sinners who are willing to confess that fact regularly in worship together.)

5. *Stop emphasizing money and contributions.* (Money is often an objectionable issue to individuals who do not feel their personal needs are being met and also to individuals who wish to suppress guilt for their lack of generosity.)
6. *Let church people be more friendly.* (How many times do strangers come and go in our midst without the regulars showing any genuine interest in them?)

According to Gallup, there is a great need among the public for spiritual moorings in life. There are large numbers of people who are hungry for a direct relationship with God. I suspect William James' long-standing observation is correct—namely, that religious experience, not theology or ceremony, is what keeps religion going. Have mainline churches, through their educational programs, become afraid of "religious experiences"? Do we find such experiences to be in opposition to scholarship and excellence?

For many, excellence smacks of elitism, and that certainly is not what I'm advocating. Snob appeal may have its place, but it is not one of the "marks" of the church. Neither, on the other hand, is mediocrity a "mark" of the church. The four traditional marks of the church are unity, sanctity, catholicity, and apostolicity. Has the church lost its zeal for upholding these benchmarks of ecclesiological excellence?

Where do you stand on the issue of excellence? Is your present attitude one of resignation when confronted with the challenge of excellence? One church member expressed his indifference by saying, "Let me have a diet drink, a television set, and for the rest, I couldn't care less." This reticent attitude on life has its moments of comfort and may even seem the sanest approach in a short life where everyone is soon forgotten. This mood of resignation is what I call the "Lazyboy" or "recliner" approach to life; its appeal is far more pervasive in our society than we are willing to admit.

At a recent ecumenical conference of clergy and laity, I heard a pastor say publicly, "We have too many lazy pastors who only do what is expected of them but nothing more." Are these pastors truly lazy, or have they simply traded in their enthusiasm for a spirit of quiet resignation to the status quo?

Stewardship as Excellence

The Christian's pursuit of excellence is theologically based on gratitude for God's grace revealed in Christ. Our physical birth and our spiritual rebirth are gifts of God's mercy. We have neither created nor earned these gifts. Having the breath of life and being given the purpose for living through Christ, we have now a new vision for the quality of life. Confronted by our nakedness at birth and death, we look upon each day as a day of grace and an opportunity to exercise our gratitude before God.

For the believer then, the *synonym for excellence is stewardship. Stewardship doesn't imply elitism but rather the wise dedication of time, talent, and resources as our response to a gracious God. Excellence is discipleship without reservations.* Is there any passion, then, to pursue this level of stewardship in our churches?

The church without a passion for excellence is dead and doesn't know it. Seminaries that cater to this inertia will die also. Unless the church and seminary together practice the politics of unconditional stewardship, there is little hope for any significant change in our midst. Becoming stewards of excellence will unlock a new chapter in the church's renewal, offering exciting opportunities to each of us who believe the church's role can be enhanced in our society.

To initiate the process toward excellence, we must begin by confronting some basic questions: (1) What mission are we in? (2) What is most central to this mission? (3) To what strategy are we committed in fulfilling this mission?

As we seek to answer these questions in our life together, we will be on the way to becoming a caring, forgiving, teaching, and creative community—moving us closer to a commitment for excellence that is contagious.

Chapter 2.
Is the Local Church a Seminary?

Do churches and seminaries share the same mission and strategy? In other words, is the local church a seminary and the seminary a church? If the passion for excellence calls for integrating the practice of ministry and theological education, then the basic similarities and dissimilarities of churches and seminaries need to be addressed.

Let's begin by asking in what ways is your church a seminary? In so far as your church or mine is a center of theological education at the grassroots, it is a seminary. Parishioners can also be viewed as "seminarians" within the larger community of the world.

In most of our churches, the theological faculty consists of one person, the pastor. Perhaps most pastors do not see themselves as grassroots theologians; the term *theologian* somehow gets restricted to seminary faculty members. But the pastor is the resident theologian of the congregation, the designated faculty member who is expected to integrate theory and practice and to comment on all the basic subjects and skills taught in a seminary curriculum.

There is, however, often a basic tension between academia and the grassroots. Seminaries unconsciously build courses around the "ideal church." For instance, the seminary offers a course—let's call it "Theology 101"; it's expected that the future pastor will translate the implications of Theology 101 into the life of the local church. This almost never is the case, since everyday experiences often defy classroom interpretations.

It seems that the more we know, the broader becomes the vast expanse of knowledge; and the more we experience, the more we realize there is much unknown to us. Our understanding lags and events seem shrouded in mystery. Our answers are, at best, partial, and our view is diffused through a veil.

This is why many suspect that the study of theology in seminary sometimes leads to ignorance at higher levels of abstraction. Ignorance and lack of certitude among grassroots theologians are really the last things the local church wants to tolerate. Parishioners believe that life's journey is difficult, and they want "simple" theological answers to life's mysteries.

Such thinking may point to anti-intellectual, antiseminary attitudes among churches. Theological education is viewed as the "enemy." This stance leads to an unreflective faith that is suspicious of any form of probing theological education.

In our attempt to protect ourselves from theological ambiguities, we are tempted to foster theological fiction that does not withstand life's realities. In practice, we influence our pastors to go through a process of "unlearning" after seminary.

The Church's Witness

On the positive side many churches are still struggling to give embodiment and concreteness to the statements declared in Theology 101. No one under the influence of Theology 101 ever graduates in the local church—not even the instructor.

The biblical standards for discipleship are always a challenge. As hesitant pilgrims, we wrestle daily in attempting to relate God's Word to the world. We find ourselves in the constant process of becoming; the journey of faith never ends, no matter how extensive our education has been.

In this process of becoming, many churchgoers show insufficient incentive for Christian growth. One pastor related to me, "The church can't be like a seminary; we simply don't have the same control as you do. We don't give evaluations. For us, pass/fail reports are left to God."

How, then, are we to evaluate the church's performance as a seminary? Admittedly, neither church nor seminary is perfect. Is there a way for each to support the ministry of the other? The linkage is not always clear.

The Seminary in the Church

It is unfortunate when theological seminaries are sometimes

viewed as the "enemy" by the grassroots; it is equally sad when seminaries view the church with suspicion.

There probably will always be a basic tension between the church's demand for accountability and the seminary's need for autonomy in pursuing its educational mission. In the midst of this tension, the church and seminary must, nevertheless, support each other.

The seminary insists on freedom to speak to the church prophetically, even when that message may be critical of the grassroots program and practice. The church, in turn, expects the seminary to graduate responsible leadership for the church; otherwise, why should churches support theological education?

Seminaries are not solely places of pure research; they are primarily teaching centers of interpretation. Seminaries serve the church best by interpreting competently the Word of God through academic disciplines and skills. One hopes the church and seminary both are committed to an educated leadership, but this fact can never be taken for granted.

Theological education must help the church to become more of a seminary in specific areas:

1. *Discipline.* Membership standards are generally slack in our churches, and the faithful core is diminishing. In the early years of Christianity, it took at least three years of disciplined faithfulness to be admitted to the household of faith. Today, we have reversed the process. It takes three years of graduate study to become an ordained pastor, while anyone can easily become a member of a congregation almost overnight.

2. *Study.* Study should be at the heart of our activities and worship services in the church. An uninformed congregation cannot possibly carry out a mission. The church as a seminary should regularly sponsor rigorous Bible study courses that meaningfully integrate theological, ethical, and pastoral concerns within the church's tradition.

3. *Prayer.* Seminarians these days talk of "spiritual formation." This should also be an essential emphasis in the life of the local church. The church as seminary must not only promote prayer among parishioners, but also assist believers to have a prayerful style of living. Our goal should be constant communication

with God, a state of mind that calls for a praying attitude in the midst of our activities and anxieties.

4. *Engagement.* The best learning takes place through engagement. Too much preaching leads to passivity, as does too much lecturing. The church as a seminary must find ways for parishioners to express and demonstrate their discipleship through relationships, advocacy opportunities, and numerous other means of social and community involvement.

Seminaries as Churches

Is the seminary *also* a church? One day a pastor came to me and said, "You are fortunate; you are with the seminary."

"Why am I so fortunate?" I asked.

"Because the seminary is not like the church," he replied.

"How is that?" I asked.

"The seminary," he went on to say, "has courses and gives grades; there's a day of reckoning at the seminary. We don't give grades at church, neither do we have an effective system of accountability foɪ our members. We are simply a volunteer organization."

Well, I hadn't quite heard the comparison between the seminary and church made in those terms before. The seminary is certainly an educational institution with standards to meet, with high expectations for students, faculty, and staff. As an accredited school, we accept the fact that criteria of accountability can be measured in quantitative and qualitative terms. The anatomy of an accredited seminary as a graduate school of higher education includes (1) experienced faculty with proper credentials, the core of any graduate institution; (2) admission standards to accept qualified students; (3) an approved curriculum and continuing education programs; (4) a good collection of library materials and related resources; (5) high academic standards; and (6) opportunities for the spiritual formation of candidates through chapel worship, study, and fellowship. Together all these aspects contribute to the community and sum up the essential components of a responsible seminary.

Seminaries, however, are special. Daily chapel services are not only a part of our spiritual formation, they actually make us unique among graduate schools of higher education. What other graduate schools include chapel services as part of their discipline? While the seminary as an educational institution can be distinguished from the church, at the same time we do not want that separation to be so broadly interpreted as to endanger the uniqueness of the seminary, embodied and symbolized in our chapel services.

The distinctiveness of theological education is its forthright confessional stance; commitment to biblical faith in a living God made flesh for us in Jesus Christ. Having confessed our bias, we are nevertheless an acknowledged partner in the academic community of graduate and professional schools. This confessional stance is the *raison d'etre* for our being and well-being.

The seminary that divorces itself from the confessing church has no future; it will lose its purpose for existence. No matter how excellent the seminary's facilities, faculty, and curriculum, the theological school that does not identify with the church has no purpose and no constituency. Some fine seminaries of the past dissolved because they lost this relationship. Other outstanding schools like Union Seminary in New York and Harvard Divinity School are consciously rebuilding bridges to the church. No seminary can trade its heritage for scarce dollars, for in the process it may lose its soul. Ministry is the main concern, and one hopes that money will follow ministry to satisfy the hard realities of our material needs.

Is the seminary, then, a church? Evidently, this simple question cannot be answered so simply. Perhaps a prior point needs to be raised; namely, what is the primary ground for our being? In other words, for whom does the seminary exist? What criteria will we use? Does the seminary exist for the students, the faculty, the board of directors, the administration, the pastors and alumni, the laity who use our facilities and participate in our programs? Who owns the seminary, not in the legal sense, but within our working consciousness? For whom does the seminary exist day in and day out? That is the questioning attitude for each of us. What perspective do you bring to the question?

From my vantage point, each group that relates to the seminary has a vested interest. Everyone who associates with the seminary community has an agenda and is willing to work for concerns within the body politic. Can we reach consensus for the grounds of our existence? In practice, do we have a common mission, and does it concur with our printed claims? Perhaps we all need to ask some fundamental questions: (1) What is a seminary? (2) Whom does it serve? (3) Why does it deserve support?

At the time of the founding of most seminaries, the above questions were raised. Take, for instance, the founding of Pittsburgh Theological Seminary in 1794 through the efforts of the Reverend John Anderson, pastor of the Service Presbyterian Church on the outskirts of Pittsburgh. Near his church there stands an inscribed stone linking the seminary with its sole instructor, Pastor Anderson. He founded the seminary to educate future leadership for the church's growth and nurture. From the very beginning, the seminary and the church were integrally related, and this continues to be the case today. Simply stated, *the seminary exists to serve the church spiritually, prophetically, intellectually, and practically in equipping men and women for ministry within and without its walls.* All support given to us reflects this explicit and implicit link between the church and seminary.

Do We Now Have an Answer to Our Question?

If the seminary primarily exists for the church, does this mean that we have reached an answer to our question? Namely, is the seminary a church? I thought so until I posed the question to a group of articulate pastors and their spouses one evening and was surprised with the direction of their thinking. Most of them responded that the seminary is not a church; they viewed the seminary through their respective images of the ideal church.

This ideal church has a sense of communion and ownership; the local congregation is a caring group of volunteers; and the church is a spiritual hospital for its members. The seminary, they concluded, is a school and not a church.

One pastor indicated that seminary education was actually a turbulent time in his life; he couldn't wait to get *into the church* and be with real people. "Today," he said, "I must confess, I feel differently. Looking back on fifteen years of ministry, I wonder now if the sharp distinction I had envisioned between the church and seminary really exists. I experienced caring people in the seminary as well as in the church, but neither institution is perfect." Our discussion ended on his note of reevaluation.

Where are you on this question? Let me share with you some of my thoughts. I am convinced that communion with God is the ultimate concern we seek to nurture through our individual experiences of faith and worship. Our experiences of worship fuel our expressions of faith. Most of our experiences of worship take place at a local church, summer camp, retreat center, etc. The experiences of awe, wonder, and conversion are the raw data that spark our individual pilgrimages. Our experience of transcendence, our moments of worship, contribute immeasurably to the primary language of faith that is locked within our inner selves. Theological education is the process of unlocking the treasure, the opportunity to reflect upon that primary experience.

The primary language of worship contains the substance that gives us cause for later reflection and discussion; without this primary substance, all theological talk within the seminary would have no reference. Theological education without worship and testimony would become an impersonal analysis of religious discourse. The seminary would become a school of religion without a confessional heart. We are, instead, God's people engaged in theologizing through our academic disciplines of Scripture, history, theology, ethics, psychology, sociology, and homiletics. In the midst of our studies, we must never cease to listen to the echo of God's Spirit beckoning us onward in our journey; doxology is our goal, even in the midst of our doubts and blind dogmatism.

Interplay of Church and Seminary

The church represents the place of our primary experience, the living laboratory for our encounters with the Divine. The seminary represents the place for critical reflection on that primary language of worship and awe. The church ushers us into mystery; the seminary probes for meaning and understanding within the context of mystery. Neither the church nor the seminary has arrived at a final destination; we are on a passage whose outcome rests with God.

The Nicene Creed characterizes the true church in terms of oneness, holiness, catholicity, and apostolicity. These qualities have often been referred to as the marks of the church, coupled with the theological virtues of faith, hope, and love. Is the seminary a church by these standards? Our answer is negative; for neither the church nor the seminary has achieved this ideal and eschatological destiny. The seminary is part of an ecumenically oriented church, and the church is part of an ecumenically oriented seminary. Both are confessionally linked together, like heart and head, listening and studying the echo of God's Spirit that challenges us all to fulfill a future greater than our vision, to reach out to the abundant life in Christ.

To sum it up: Is the seminary a church? *Yes, the seminary is the* ecclesia, *the People of God, at study and self-reflection on the church's worship and witness in the world. The church is also the seminary at the grassroots, translating the language of worship into action.* Neither can exist without the other; neither can afford to become possessive or distant from the other, the integral ties must be consciously strengthened. Each subsidizes the other in fulfilling our common mission of service in the name of Christ who empowers us to practice faith, hope, and love. Together we are the Body of Christ propelled by the vision of God each of us has claimed. With God's help, let us pursue our common journey toward the unending source of Light and Life.

Churches can help seminaries to be more vital in the following ways:

First, the local congregation must help the seminary to balance criticism with charity. The church often accepts people's frailties more easily than do seminarians and faculties. The emphasis on forgiveness at the grassroots must also be witnessed in the seminary classroom beyond a discussion topic.

Second, the local church can teach the seminary the cost of discipleship. During the seminary period, we become conditioned to receiving, and, at times, not enough genuine sharing takes place. Basic to any sharing is the need to listen and hear one another's concerns. Seminaries must also share materially, no matter how limited our resources.

It is truly meaningful when our seminarians take the initiative to give from their meager budgets for the hungry and oppressed in the world, as many do during the course of an academic year. Only through genuine giving of self and substance can we establish community.

Third, there is, at times, greater tolerance for Christian diversity in local churches than in some seminary communities. In seminaries, we often utter considerable lip service to diversity, while seeking conformity. Games are played among seminarians to test one another's orthodoxy.

We must move beyond such testing and learn to live beyond our labels, discovering the authenticity of one another's Christian witness. Field education plays a key role as it offers students a glimpse of the local church at its best and at its worst. Through proper guidance, these field-based experiences are among the most important "seminary classrooms" for demonstrating loving tolerance in the midst of diversity.

The church is a seminary, but neither the seminary nor the church has lived up to its potential. The mandate is clear: churches must point to seminaries and seminaries to churches, each learning from the other what it lacks, as both seek to be more effective and excellent in their respective missions.

Only through mutual exchange can we hope to uphold "the priesthood of all believers," in which we all are called to be ministers and interpreters of God's redeeming grace.

Chapter 3.
The Challenge of John 3:16 for Church and Seminary

I came across a Chinese fortune cookie recently that disappointed me. I don't know about you, but I enjoy cracking open that fortified treasure after a Chinese meal. On this occasion there was no promise of wealth, happiness, and fame; instead I found a proverb of six words: "We learn little and forget much." I think this proverb was especially aimed for seminary presidents in particular; perhaps it could be applied to seminarians and then even reach some church members! According to this proverb, there is very little knowledge retained, and so let us briefly examine the tiny nuggets surviving our common pilgrimage of faith.

For many Christians our knowledge can be summed up in John 3:16 (RSV): "For God so loved the world that he gave his only Son, that whoever believes in him should not perish, but have eternal life." This is probably the most memorized verse of Scripture that most Christians carry with them. The summary of the gospel contained in this verse is the one piece of news that the church has found fit to proclaim in every generation since the advent of Christ.

What challenge does John 3:16 hold for today's church and for theological education? Has the urgency of this verse escaped our attention? Perhaps our response has been buried in all the knowledge we have acquired and partially digested in our hurry to graduate from the educational process. We have forgotten the fact that no one ever graduates from being a student of faith, especially those of us who teach the faith.

The church stands today, as it always has, between the advent reported in John 3:16 and a changing world. Visit any historical museum and you can see that the world changes; there are layers of civilization that have risen and fallen through the centuries. In the midst of this historical process, the church's mission is to interpret the event of Jesus Christ and to intercede in his name to a world materially and spiritually in need.

The primary task of a theological seminary, as a graduate school of the church, is to provide educated leadership for the church in fulfilling her mission. Our specific task is to graduate astute interpreters and doers of the Word of God in a clamoring world.

As Christ was sent, so too are we commissioned to go forth under the sign of his cross into the marketplaces of contemporary society, equipped to tell the story encapsuled in the text of John 3:16.

Yet, quite honestly, we feel powerless when confronted by the worldly context that faces Christians everywhere on this planet. The sights, sounds, and smells of this world are not always pleasant; nor can they be caught accurately on our television screens. The raw realities are intimidating, even crushing at times, eclipsing the tiny oasis of hope wherever two, three, or more are gathered in his name. A day doesn't go by that we aren't caught struggling with our love/hate emotions toward the world.

At times we are at a loss to know just how to respond as we fight for survival. Others of us are so preoccupied with skirmishes within our homes, churches, and seminary communities that we haven't even the energy to do battle with the larger issues of our society. Our current tendency toward spiritual inwardness in the life of the church may be a sign of our poor health. We are losing sight of the larger world that God loves. My travels in the United States and abroad have impressed upon me the ghetto mentality that prevails in our Christian communities.

Do you recall the street scenes in the film *Passage to India?* I felt I was living that experience several times as we visited the marketplaces of Seoul, Hong Kong, and especially Cairo. During one incident, an Egyptian pastor led me on foot from his church located in a worker's district of Cairo to the train station a short distance away. It was only a twenty-five minute walk but one of the most exotic pathways of my life. The sights, sounds, and smells surrounding me were an unbelievable cacophony to behold. While preoccupied with the physical safety of my-self and others, I was momentarily "lost" in the multitude of humanity pressing in upon me, shouting and struggling for their slice of life. How in God's name can anyone proclaim John 3:16 to this unruly mob and expect a hearing? The scene before me did violence to my sense of balance; this very real but foreign world upset my psychic equilibrium. You may have found yourself reacting similarly or in another way to this strange scene.

The point I want to make is that most of our twentieth-century theology originated on the cleanly swept streets of Basel, Zurich, Edinburgh, Tubingen, and Marburg; a long distance physically and psychologically from the crowded cities and alleyways of Seoul, Hong Kong, Cairo, and Bombay. Can these theologies of the Occident really apply to non-Western societies where the vast majority of the world's population resides? Where are we tackling this question in our seminary curriculums in the West?

How in the world can the love of God wrap itself around this entire globe of ours? There is, I'm convinced, an inherent mystery to the width, length, and depth of God's love in Jesus Christ. The biblical reality is that God loves this world of ours and all its humanity; the more difficult issue confronting us is whether we do. Or are we in large measure expending our energies to protect ourselves from the real world, hiding within the sanctuaries of our middle-class homes and suburban shop-ping centers?

We already know that affluent Christians are a minority among the world's poor, Christians and non-Christians. What we are not so willing to admit is that the majority of the world's people out there are simply too frightening a reality for us. This is true even for our faithful missionaries who live at times by double standards just as we do, giving voice to the oppressed and poor but requiring, like us, middle-class standards of shelter in order to maintain a sense of security. My intention here is not to be judgmental toward anyone but to point out the dilemma in which we find ourselves—on the one hand, we are challenged to love and accept the world as God does; yet on the other hand, we are aware that oppressive conditions and dirty surroundings weaken our resolve and undermine our witness. This may be precisely why we admire Mother Teresa, Bishop Tutu, and others who compensate for our limited commitment. I suspect the number of truly dedicated believers around the globe is rather small.

The Challenge to Seminaries

What can we do to raise our level of commitment today? This is the paramount question facing theological education when all is said and done. Are we willing to become church leaders who will make a difference? Are we willing to be more demanding of ourselves? Are we willing to work as diligently as our rhetoric claims? There is, I'm afraid, far more complacency and laziness in our church and seminary communities than we are willing to admit. We seem to want rewards and recognition whenever we do something "extra" for Jesus. At times we confuse our discipleship with our compensation package. Perhaps Jürgen Moltmann is correct when he suggests that today's Christianity demands nothing. The product of organized Christianity today is an institutionalized absence of commitment. A Christianity without demands points to a church without vitality; it suggests an irrelevant gospel that is largely ignored in the marketplaces of the world.

We must not only recommit ourselves to become leaders who will make a difference in our churches and societies, but we must begin with ourselves, not our neighbors. Furthermore, we must be willing to widen our circles of concern. But does the church want leadership that loves the real world? Or is our primary interest in leaders who will comfort us rather than challenge us? Obviously we need both! The issue is whether the church wants to encourage challenging and creative leadership to develop and to confront the status quo? Does the church desire leadership that is willing to risk for the world that God loves? Accepting the world around us is the first major hurdle most of us may have to overcome. My guess is that each of us needs to wrestle with this issue in private with the One who is our Creator, Redeemer, and Sustainer.

The prevailing attitude I see at home and abroad is to maintain the status quo. This point of view is turning our churches into museums. We can't blame communism or our respective theologies on the fact that our churches are declining in membership. We have more steeples dedicated to God in our cities and countrysides now than I care to count. At the same time we have communities with unchurched people who no longer feel the need to attend our sparsely filled churches, which they find irrelevant and unexciting. Even our best attended churches in the United States have less than half of their membership attending regularly. The causes for our decline are many, but the key to turning the situation around lies with committed leadership in partnership with a laity willing to work creatively and courageously.

One Korean pastor asked me a probing question during my lectures a few years ago at Yonsei University in Seoul. He asked, "How can you come and tell us how to revitalize our churches when the churches in your own country are declining?" This is certainly a fair question to put to an American. Christianity is expanding in his country and in Africa but waning in Europe and in the United States. How would you respond to such an earnest question?

I wonder if our churches are willing to tolerate aggressive and visionary leadership to turn us around? Perhaps instead we would prefer a church of housekeeping managers who are called upon to administer what our forebears have created?

Two basic questions face the American church today. First, does the church want leadership? And second, do we want to be leaders? These are the two recurring questions that keep surfacing before me. The resurgence of fundamentalism today is due in part to the leadership vacuum among our mainline churches, which have become preoccupied with maintaining their structures rather than expanding their capacity to take risks. Evangelism is not valid unless we are willing to involve ourselves meaningfully into the lives of others we are seeking to reach.

We must remind ourselves continually that the church and the seminary that understand their mission are committed always to a permanent reformation—*ecclesia reformata et semper reformanda.* The "church reformed and always reforming" is the hallmark of our heritage. Frankly, without a reforming bias, there is no way for us to fulfill the challenge of John 3:16 before an intimidating world.

We in the seminaries need to wrestle more vigorously with the text of John 3:16 through our course work, times of fellowship, and during the countless dialogue opportunities that occur on and off campus. We must become more astute students of society, beginning with our immediate neighborhoods, as we seek to grasp the social and economic dimensions of the community as well as the belief systems that compete within us. We must exert a greater effort to understand the local marketplace with all of the sights, sounds, and smells if meaningful communication is to take place.

The Challenge to the Churches

The church worldwide sees itself as the *primary international community of moral discourse,* seeking to be a cosmopolitan conscience that calls us beyond parochialism and nationalism. Nations tend to build walls of security and protection, insulating citizens from global realities. Protectionism is more than an issue of economic trade; it is a myopic attitude of nations that foolishly consider their people as the only ones who count. We know this isn't so, but too often we draw a circle around our self-interests. Essential to the church's mission is broadening our understanding of self-interest to correspond with global realities. No nation in today's interconnected world can survive in isolation.

The church realized the oneness of our existence long before telecommunication, airplanes, and space travel. The mandate to the first Christians in the Great Commission called them to reach out to the whole inhabited world and beyond. Thus looking to the future, we must practice a threefold theology of mission.

The *first dimension of a mission theology is hospitality,* which has been integral to our history. Henri Nouwen put it well in his book *Reaching Out,* emphasizing that it is obligatory for all Christians to offer open and hospitable space where strangers can cast off their strangeness and become fellow human beings.

I have experienced hospitality on numerous travels abroad, gratefully recalling kindnesses in Switzerland, India, Iran, East Germany, the Soviet Union, Romania, Japan, Korea, and Egypt. My gracious hosts included Christians and non-Christians. May

God inspire us to show greater hospitality to a world now on the doorstep of local churches through colleges and universities with international students. In any single year, over 345,000 international students from nearly two hundred countries are on U.S. campuses. Local churches can take the initiative by arranging annual international weekends, inviting these students to their churches and homes.

The *second dimension is understanding,* which always involves information, reflection, and engagement. Where there is understanding, dialogue is enriched and the opportunities for cooperation increase. To invite and support an overseas Christian leader as a missionary-in-residence to your congregation is one way to increase that valuable understanding.

The *third dimension is inclusiveness.* God is not preoccupied with structures, institutions, or property; God's attention is centered on people (John 3:16). As we grasp the meaning of God's great love for the world through Christ, we will come to a profound commitment to the *imago dei*—the "image of God" found in every human being. It is this *imago dei* that enables us to relate to others. In this caring context we share and learn from one another. Finding ways to connect with others is the mandate implicit in the challenge of John 3:16.

A threefold mission theology of hospitality, understanding, and inclusiveness really has a single focus—namely, *to honor and love God through everyone.* As the church becomes more inclusive in outlook, at home and abroad, we will find ourselves supporting a Christianity without boundaries. Ministry with a global perspective faces the future without fear, encouraged to take bolder risks in a technologically shrinking planet. The future belongs to God, and we are privileged to participate, however modestly, in that future.

Our calling is clear: we are expected both to interpret and to be involved in this world. The church is the vehicle by which we carry out the mandate of John 3:16. Let's move ahead in confidence, knowing that the cross of Christ has gone before us and the strength of God's spirit is behind us. However, are we willing to accept and love the world as God did in Jesus Christ?

Unfortunately, the Chinese proverb is true: we will learn little and forget much during our pilgrimage. But we hope that the simplicity and urgency of John 3:16 will stick with us and motivate us. God, indeed, loved the world and sent Jesus even to the cross that each of us might experience the fullness of life now and always.

Chapter 4.

Toward a Common Curriculum for Parish and Classroom

To meet the challenge of John 3:16, there ought to be a basic curriculum for the parish and classroom. Do the church and seminary share a common curriculum?

"What do you learn in seminary?" a college student asked me recently. Well, of course, I could answer that we completely master Hebrew and Greek, analyze the Bible and theological dogmatics from cover to cover, become prophets in the pulpit, and finely hone our counseling skills.

Instead, our conversation covered a more realistic range of subjects. The student noted that various graduate schools are easily categorized by their intended mission—for instance, a medical school is associated with healing and acquiring diagnostic skills; a law school is interested in interpreting regulations and the rights of citizens within due process; business schools are concerned with profit-making and management; and an engineering school with precision calculations and projects. But what is the main thrust of the seminary? And, for that matter, what is the main thrust of the church?

Today's seminarian is not interested in being simply a keeper of the institutional church. My personal observation is that today's seminarians are eager to transform society and to breathe new life into the organizational church.

It is true that religious institutions have declined in the past decades, but many of us recognize new stirrings, and increased diversity of enrollment may be an early sign of renewal. During the 1990s, a clergy shortage is even projected. According to Martin Marty of the *Christian Century,* three out of every five Americans continue to support religious-related institutions, and two out of five Americans participate regularly in worship services. The pastor, if he or she chooses, is still an important voice and opinion-maker within the community; religion is certainly not dead in American life. Clergy have a significant job of interpretation at the grassroots level; this brings us to the basic task and purpose of the seminary and church. How does the seminary equip pastors for their responsibilities, and, in turn, how do pastors equip parishioners for informed service in the church and society?

Theological seminaries are schools of interpretation. The seminary is a hermeneutical center based upon a traditional fourfold curricular structure featuring the disciplines of Bible, theology, church history, and practical theology. Variations and subspecialties are built around this basic fourfold structure called a "theological encyclopedia."

Theologian Edward Farley of Vanderbilt University, in his book entitled *Theologia,* charges that seminary education under this fourfold paradigm has lost any semblance of theological coherence. There is no common theological understanding among the various disciplines of a seminary faculty. There doesn't seem to be any common end or purpose that unifies theological education today. There is a plurality of agenda without any dialogue taking place. Like many congregations, seminary faculties are polite, congenial, and seek to avoid conflict; thus, most faculty members tend to work in isolation from one another. Farley makes a plea for dialogue and theological coherence but does not suggest what the content of this theological unity might be. This is a task for every seminary community to struggle with, discuss, and debate among ourselves. Such an exercise can be healthy for theological education seeking a clear self-image as a graduate professional school.

The question, "What do we learn in seminary?" finds its answers through the curriculum. Developing a curriculum is primarily a responsibility of the faculty, but input is also needed from others interested in the future of the seminary and church. The objective of the curriculum is to graduate people for a learned pastoral ministry, which in turn presupposes a learned faculty.

Unfortunately, there continues to be a gap today between learning and doing in seminary life. Both are essential, but frankly we sometimes try to practice before proper study and are guilty of pastoral malpractice. No professional can practice in the field without knowing the basic anatomy of their discipline. The seminary is more than a "how-to" school; it is primarily a school of interpretation of the gospel message. One effective way to combat church decline is to reduce theological malpractice by providing well-prepared practitioners laboring within the Body of Christ.

However, to be a learned clergy dependent upon a learned faculty is not enough. We need a unifying purpose to fuse our intellect and piety together for action. We need to recover a common theological base for reflection and action as believers. The college student was really asking me a fundamental question when he inquired, "What do you learn in seminary?" To state it another way, what does theological education offer society? What unique skills are acquired from the seminary that have credibility within secular society? What are we proposing to accomplish in theological education? What can the faculty, administration, and trustees promise seminarians and supporters? Only a curriculum with clear intention will prepare graduates for their practice of ministry. Choosing and defining this intention ought to be an exciting concern in every seminary and local church.

Permit me to begin this definition of curriculum by stating to you my own bias. I propose that the common curriculum for church and seminary ought to be found within the theme of "forgiveness." The goal of a theological curriculum in the church and seminary is to educate seminarians and parishioners who have a realistic grasp on what the power of forgiveness can do in an unforgiving society. The factor of forgiveness is a missing ingredient in this world bent on narrow self-interest and the capacity for self-destruction. The practice of forgiveness enhances the quality of all life and rehumanizes our existence with dignity.

Toward a Curriculum of Forgiveness

Perhaps we ought to bestow graduates with a master's degree in forgiveness, rather than divinity. This might more accurately describe what our daily objective as Christians ought to be. How can you and I go through a week of living without being a part of the forgiving process—bringing renewal and reconciliation to our fragmented society? The essence of the Christian faith is forgiveness. Christ is forgiveness in the flesh; can there be a more satisfying explanation of the incarnation than that? Forgiving one another is the human way of loving; it is a liberating means of experiencing fulfillment and joy.

Do you think that forgiveness is neither realistic nor applicable in an unfair and unjust world? I have sometimes felt that way. At times forgiveness seems an anemic approach to the harsh realities and power politics of organizations and nations. Even so, can you imagine what the quality of life would be like without forgiveness? The answer is hell. Living in a vengeful and suspicious global island is a hellish existence, where forgiveness is sometimes experienced as an alien accident in human life.

We can discuss peacemaking into eternity, but without forgiveness the propensity for revenge will continue to outweigh the urgency for reconciliation. Frankly, we haven't progressed much from the ancient adage of "an eye for an eye, and a tooth for a tooth." Today's car sticker puts it this way: "Bumper to Bumper and I'll get you." Translate that into social, economic, and political terms on our global sandlot and we can understand the tensions headlining our daily news reports. Have the shootings of the Korean and Iranian jetliners already slipped into the background of our memory? Are you aware of the untold thousands of innocent men, women, and children who have died violently in recent years in Nicaragua? What about refugees from El Salvador, Afghanistan, South Africa, Lebanon, Uganda, Cambodia, and elswhere? Let's not forget the needs of numerous displaced workers who are victims of global competition and technological change. Also, we have an aging population threatened by rising costs, the increasing battle for basic rights of women, minorities, and disabled people. Does the word *forgiveness* sound weak and ineffective to remedy these realities?

In fact, some observers wonder if the church and theological education under any theme are designed to cope with the real world. Theological communities, it seems, have themselves found theological language inadequate; they sometimes adopt the terms and causes of current events such as liberation, feminization, democratic socialism, democratic capitalism, individualism, communitarianism, self-actualization, etc. In the marketplace of ideas, theological insight is often buried under a bushel of ideologies; the social pronouncements of ecclesiastical organizations simply echo modified versions of the Democratic and Republican party platforms.

The uniqueness of the church's witness is lost among the prevailing moods of society; as a consequence, the seminary is often bombarded to add courses reflecting various deficiencies in society. Simply put, we can lose control of the curriculum. We sometimes trade off basic subjects in order to provide Band-Aids for the wounds of society, in our efforts to be relevant. Ironically, our attempt to solve problems by adding courses to the crowded curriculum still leaves us with insufficient "right" courses. At the same time, so few students are able to sign up for the elective courses offered that faculty feel it is time for another curriculum revision. And so, the game of curriculum change is played once again. Professor Farley laments this absence of cohesive theological formation within the curriculum. Instead, the process of addition fosters a dispersed curriculum, pushing many seminary faculty members into their specific interests, becoming strangers to one another. One seminary dean is especially urging each faculty member to read the books of colleagues so that dialogue within the academic halls might again take place. A sense of cohesive structure cannot be relegated to a congenial atmosphere of uncritical tolerance.

You may be questioning, as I am at this point, whether a theological curriculum ought to have a single focus. The faculty of Pittsburgh Seminary has responded to that question already in adopting a one-year experimental study on the impact of peacemaking upon the seminary curriculum. The faculty was willing to take such a risk. Perhaps we need to go further and focus on the numerous dimensions of "forgiveness." Does this term adequately reach the essence of our biblical heritage symbolized by the cross of Christ?

From my perspective forgiveness is the necessary premise for any sustaining effort at peacemaking. There is no *shalom* without forgiveness. To live by the forgiveness of God without forgiving one's enemy is inconceivable. This fact is true for people, organizations, and nations. Forgiveness is not only a substantive matter in Christian theology, it can be the most durable thread from which theological education receives unity and strength. God's forgiveness and human forgiveness are intimately interwoven (Matthew 5 and 18). Baptism, eucharist, and penance are mediating channels by which divine forgiveness is expressed. The climactic prayer of Jesus on the cross for the forgiveness of his enemies (Luke 23:34) highlights divine power and human need at the same time. Forgiveness comes from God and has the power to reconcile not only people but also classes, nations, and races. We have only experienced a glimpse of the potential that comes in power and reconciliation through forgiveness.

Yet the question persists, will a focus on forgiveness educate us for the "real world"? Sometimes, more often than we are willing to admit, our desire to be in the real world is only a position of rhetoric; we tend actually to favor those examples and leaders that reinforce our biases and prejudices based upon earlier notions and myths that are no longer relevant. We nurture romantic illusions of the past and challenge new viewpoints. Leadership directed toward reality is today's need and a specific challenge for us in theological education. In his book *The American Disease,* George C. Lodge claims that the American predisposition to deny reality is the American disease. We create a fictional existence by living yesterday's formulations in a changing world. We become creatures of contradiction, singing out lustily the hymns of the past while cheating to survive in a world that we don't acknowledge.

Flying the Flag of Forgiveness from Our Steeples

Only forgiveness will enable us to be touched with the healing realities of our hymns as we encounter the real world of daily events. We do indeed live east of Eden. Forgiveness accepts the reality of sin, a reality often denied in our sophisticated but disillusioned society. We try to lessen the sting of sin and dilute our need for forgiveness. We search for an endless list of panaceas to rationalize our shortcomings, while society continues to be suspicious, vengeful, and unforgiving. The divine prescription of forgiveness has yet to be adopted by the majority. We often reject the painful struggle necessary before genuine forgiveness and renewal can be a vital part of our lives and communities. How can we get this message across?

The church and seminary can begin by providing leadership educated for reality, by integrating forgiveness into the curriculum and into our community life. We must realize at the same time that forgiveness involves a price of pain.

The seminary is more than a sanctuary for scholarship; it is also a center for the practice of forgiveness. During the student's first year of study, a conscious effort could be made to exegete the theme of forgiveness in biblical courses as well as introductory studies in other disciplines. Many dimensions to forgiveness need to be studied and digested. In the second year, a field-based course could be proposed to integrate the history, theology, ethics, and spirituality of forgiveness with explicit emphasis on how local churches can become centers of forgiveness. In the actual life of the parish, problems of forgiveness are not separated into courses but come in complex and unexpected packages. In the senior year, small-group seminars under faculty leadership could focus on probing, through case studies, the enemies of forgiveness, such as power, property, pluralism, and pride. Unchecked political power denies its own blindness and dehumanizes life; turf issues and questions of property have torn up more families, businesses, and nations than we can recount. Uncritical pluralism can ultimately deny the goal of human unity and become demonic under the guise of tolerance. Pride, national and personal, can cause us to lose our objective perspective on our weaknesses and need for interdependence.

A three-year core curriculum on forgiveness in our seminaries is one way to restore the needed theological coherence within our historic fourfold curricular structure. Churches that develop and regularly repeat a basic class on forgiveness will have a constant reminder of their essential mission in society. Such an emphasis would encourage us to become practicing disciples of forgiveness in a fragmented world.

Unpacking the meaning and significance of forgiveness has

biblical, theological, and ethical significance for society as well as the church. This is the time for individuals as well as for the organized structures of our society to seriously consider the renewing options provided by the practice of forgiveness in all phases of our lives.

Chapter 5.

Beyond Burnout:
The Journey to Renewal

A curriculum of forgiveness will direct us to the constant need for renewal and reform within our churches and seminaries. We hope the journey to renewal will take us beyond burnout in the pew and pulpit.

There is much talk today on the renewal of the church. Renewal appears to be a code term for whatever is seen as a deficiency in the church's doctrine and practice. The synonyms for renewal are many, each reflecting someone's or some group's agenda for the church. The bottom line for all renewal discussion points to a basic question—What is really needed for the church to be the church today? What new theological or ecclesiastical garment will hide our past errors and fashionably bring us into a new era of rebirth? Frankly, I question whether any new garment is needed at all.

I attended the World Council of Churches Sixth Assembly in Vancouver, Canada. One day following lunch, I and an Eastern Orthodox professor from Eastern Europe were walking on the campus of the University of British Columbia, the site of the assembly. We asked some Canadians for directions to the path leading down to the beach. The university is situated on an elevated plateau with a sandy beach located below the forest and cliffs. The area is beautiful; I don't know what the Garden of Eden was like, but Vancouver can't be far behind.

We descended the cliff through a forest of trees and shrubbery without seeing the shoreline until we suddenly came upon it and discovered to our utter amazement that we were on a well-populated nudist beach. What a shock for two straight-laced theologians from the East and West!

The surprising experience highlighted for me how inhibited and conditioned my life has been. To suddenly come upon a contemporary version of the biblical garden, indeed, took me off stride. I suspect the same may be true for you. It certainly requires a new level of consciousness and liberation; a journey, I'm afraid, I'm not ready to make as yet.

Why do I share this incident with you? Simply to illustrate that the need for renewal among our churches and institutions also calls for a shocking rebirth of attitudes and outlooks so entrenched in each of us that we aren't able in reality to go beyond the rhetoric of renewal. We must confess that it is difficult to push beyond talk to the experience awaiting us unless we shed theological and ideological garments so firmly fixed to our skins, preventing us from having a fresh perspective and vision from God. Indeed, we live east of Eden! Our sinfulness has dulled our imagination and curtailed our capacity to act. The winds of the Spirit of God have yet to force us out of our fortresses.

Renewal for me does not mean the addition of theological phrases, labels, or confessions but the actual shedding of our ecclesiastical garments as we uncover the roots of our beginning. We need to remind ourselves that we stand physically and theologically naked before God at every crucial point of our lives—from birth to death. Nothing is hidden from the divine presence. My Bible is clear on that point! God knows my private as well as my public agenda. Without risking the loss of our garments of security—pet ideas, theologies, territorial rights, and material treasures—what chance has any of us to enter into the reality of renewal beyond rhetoric? Are we too heavily laden with wardrobes to make any real progress in our journey as pilgrims? Without an honest admission that there are simply too many garments weighing us down, we can't even begin our journey in faithfulness to the God who has called and commissioned us in Jesus Christ.

The task of theological education, whether in our seminaries or in our churches, is to break down these visible and invisible layers that cause us so much frustration, anxiety, and despair. We need to move out into the wider world waiting to be discovered. Why are we so content with our burdens? It's a great puzzle to me. The freedom we enjoy in Christ is to break away, to cut loose the leashes held by limited theologies, dogmatic individuals, and ecclesiastical structures and to discover the fact that in Christ we have handed over leadership to a gracious God who has extended our radius of outreach, encouraging us to move beyond our crowded towers of Babel and become pilgrims pointed to a promised land under a new covenant in Christ.

The Church's Call

What is the mandate of this new covenant in Christ? Has the church's history ever indicated a clear consensus regarding its mission and purpose on earth? I am afraid not! The interpretative or hermeneutical struggle continues now and will continue into the indefinite future. There never seems to be a confessional statement made within the church without dissent. Within the household of faith there will always exist a variety of interpretations concerning the mission of the church and the requirements to fulfill that mission. Every ecclesiastical community seems to have an answer for the church's renewal.

At present, evangelical Christians insist on an uncompromised proclamation of the gospel, baptizing men and women in the good news of Jesus Christ, as the answer for church renewal. What is missing, they feel, is the proper emphasis on evangelism in the church.

Charismatic Christians point to Scripture and declare that our mission is to grasp God's gifts to us, baptizing men and women in the power of the Holy Spirit. What is missing, from their perspective, is emphasis on the Spirit's power not only to transform lives but to heal bodies as well. Herein lies their answer for the church's renewal.

Liberation Christians also point to Scripture and declare that the church's mission is to identify and support the poor and the oppressed, working toward a kingdom of God consisting of peace and justice. What is missing, from their viewpoint, is a prophetic proclamation backed by relevant social deeds.

Enlightened evangelicals, charismatics, and liberationists in their various ways realize that all of the above emphases need to be made without the exclusion of one or the other. A majority of Christians are searching for a wholistic witness. The assembly of the World Council of Churches at Vancouver noted this wholistic approach, calling for a synthesis of peace *and* justice, salvation *and* power in its theme: "Jesus Christ—The Life of the World."

However, the implementation of a wholistic witness is not at all easy. The means of implementation divides Christians globally today. The issue of uniting means and ends is the ecumenical task of the hour. Realistic Christians cannot separate means from ends; such a separation would violate the significance of a wholistic approach in our Christian witnessing. Whatever the conflict, the resolution of the problem needs to keep the means and ends before us closely related. Means determine ends, and ends determine means; this is an integral principle of wholistic witnessing.

Jesus was attempting to teach his disciples this lesson when Peter sliced off the ear of the servant to the high priest during that fateful hour before the crucifixion. Can God's kingdom be born out of violence? Or for that matter, can God's kingdom be born without violence? What does the cross of Christ actually symbolize for believers—violence or nonviolence? This is an unresolved focus of tension within today's household of faith.

It is incumbent on Christians—EAST, WEST, NORTH, and SOUTH—to develop an adequate theology of means and ends if we are to transcend the current divisions and suspicions in our international community. To contrast sharply in our rhetoric between oppressors and oppressed in a dynamically changing world is naive. The roles can become reversed overnight. To advocate nuclear disarmament unilaterally over limited disarmament is another case in point. Most of us are more than willing to become nuclear pacifists yet in the same breath confess the need and even the justification to equip our police forces with guns to respond to our domestic concerns. Is there ever an easy answer to our moral dilemmas? No scriptural interpretation is absolute in its understanding of God's will. Each of us is left with a personal struggle of conscience; we must come to terms with our aggressive instincts as we wave our flags of peace.

The fundamental task of any renewal concern is to help the church to become reacquainted with its roots. The church must shed many garments, clean out attics and cellars, rid itself of excess baggage collected over the decades, and discover true essence. Without a determination to confront our heritage, we will bounce around endlessly, responding to contemporary crises by organizing and reorganizing institutional structures.

Exactly how afield are we from the mission of the Founder? It seems we have allowed the pluralism of our world society to define our agenda and to stifle our enthusiasm for change. That is to say, we have surrendered to the complexity of our global village and become frozen into a status quo position. Jesus, for all practical purposes, is no longer our Messiah; rather, whoever or whatever enables us to survive or guarantees our tenure a bit longer is "the saviour of the moment," receiving our loyalty and support. In our reflective moments we become cynical; we know that we are *all* oppressed, and yet we continue to allow ourselves to be victimized by the impersonal forces of poverty and affluence, by greed, pride, and power. We are all in need of liberation—the need for renewal encompasses us all; each of us has a case history of hurts and hopes to bring to the theological journey toward renewal.

Your starting point biblically, theologically, and ethically may differ from your neighbor, but each of us must at least encourage the other in love to theologize from a global stance in the name of Christ. In truth we are all beginners and can learn from each other. No one, I find, has "arrived" as a Christian. We are all sojourners—this is what it means to be a pilgrim community, for the seminary as well as for the neighborhood church. We all need to discover our mission, the *raison d'être* of our existence. This discovery will release a flow of energy and enthusiasm to affect every nook and cranny of our lives and communities. We will become Christians with a purpose; and Christians who have a purpose beyond mere survival have the power to move mountains. Believers with purpose can move beyond burnout. It is when we lose our sense of spiritual direction and vision (calling) that we are in danger of burnout.

Anatomy of Renewal

Finally, let me share, in broad strokes, the basic structure of a renewal theology that churches and seminaries can share in common. To begin with, the heart of a theology of renewal is a conscious dependence upon the Holy Spirit. Only through the

Spirit will we experience the power of Jesus' ministry to tear down the walls of separation and to lift our horizons toward God's vision for us.

A renewal theology needs also to encapsule a biblical image of the kingdom of God, a dream of the promised land where life can become fully human. For me, that biblical image is the Garden of Eden. What was it like? None of us really knows; we all have bits and pieces of the grand picture. Let's exercise our theological imagination together as we seek to understand the quality of life in the Garden of Eden. As we share our visions and hopes, we need to step out and test the best approaches (means) in making our journey. How we meld together our means and our ends will be the most difficult task of our journey. The pilgrimage toward the garden of God, that sacred place of peace, justice, and personal fulfillment—salvation in its total-ity—needs to involve the combined effort of all people—EAST, WEST, NORTH, and SOUTH. To do less makes no sense to a pilgrim Christian.

A renewal theology will also have a sense of discipline. Discipleship means discipline. Theological education is one form of discipline. Physical discipline along with spiritual and intellectual discipline are necessary efforts to travel the pilgrim's route. In the final analysis, a renewal theology depends on a network of people who are willing to support one another in prayer and through concrete deeds. This network is the nervous system of renewal that keeps the Body of Christ alive and sensitive to the larger world that needs our services.

The journey to renewal does not depend, then, on creating a new shopping list of ecclesiastical accessories or devising trendy theological labels but rather calls for a radical reduction of all theological and nontheological vestments that prevent us from marching in the unencumbered style of pilgrims, dis-covering the total contents of our global island. I wonder if any church or ecclesiastical tradition is truly prepared to make a journey toward renewal, risking both substance and status in the process. Unless we are willing to lay aside all garments of seeming importance, we are not yet ready physically, mentally, or emotionally to commence on a pilgrimage. Until we are wil-ling to be freed of needless garments we have not yet followed

Jesus' example to forsake all and enter into communion with God.

Before you and I can fulfill our calling to be pilgrims, we must in faith be willing to strip away whatever is holding us back, by (1) getting in touch with our roots; (2) discovering anew our dependence on the Holy Spirit; (3) sharing a common vision of God's garden; (4) developing a disciplined program of preparation; and (5) nurturing an ecumenical network of people whose resources and services are generously open to one another's disposal. To this end seminaries, particularly through their continuing education programs, can assist grassroots churches.

We would all like to see renewal and resurrection among our churches and denominations. We know it will take more than three days. Our focus for the immediate future ought to be centered on a program of disciplined nurture and enthusiastic outreach to the unchurched.

Harvard historian William Hutchison indicates that the established Protestant denominations are becoming a minority movement and must accept sectarian status. Mainline denominations are becoming today's "oldliners." The average membership age is near fifty and over in these established churches. Maturing denominations are facing a serious problem that cannot be ignored. Our three-year Aging Project at Pittsburgh Seminary focused on this problem and its implications for theological education. If the replacement levels of members do not increase, we could well become a vanishing denomination in the twenty-first century.

What can we do about it? The politics of resurrection call for vigorous effort at the local church level. *First* and foremost, every congregation ought to analyze their situation *realistically*. *Second,* develop prayer and Bible study circles throughout your congregation, studying especially the Book of Acts. How eager are we to have God's Spirit blowing in our midst?

Third, organize a strategy for outreach based on reliable community data and gather people together who are excited about the church's mission. Form this core of committed people as an outreach group and call them the *Committee of Seventy-Two* (Luke 10:1–20). In situations where you might have less than "seventy-two" committed persons in your local church, then make "seventy-two" the initial target to be reached by your core group. *Fourth,* develop an engaging program of Christian education for all ages. Bringing new people to church without offering substantive nurture in discipleship is foolish.

Fifth, attempt to have everyone at church placed into some meaningful fellowship with others. Fellowship bonded by trust and love in the name of Christ is essential to church building. *Sixth,* fuel your fellowship through service that addresses human needs. Such opportunities for service will also enhance the church's prophetic witness and relevance within the community.

The journey to renewal and excellence is a never-ending task for a pilgrim church no longer satisfied with rhetoric; it is the sanctifying process for which we have been justified in Christ. By God's grace, we are led step by step toward the garden, to feast someday at God's picnic table awaiting us at journey's end.

Chapter 6.

Characteristics of Excellence in Clergy Leadership

The journey to renewal and rebirth leads to the crucial issue of clergy leadership. What are the characteristics of excellence in leadership? Concensus on this matter is pivotal in our pursuit of excellence in the churches and seminaries.

Having *trust* in clergy leadership is essential for any successful prescription to restore power and momentum among *mainline churches.* Where there is trust, leadership is empowered to lead. Where trust is missing, we find ourselves meeting, and meeting, and meeting, until committee sessions exhaust us into a state of indecision. Trust is not established overnight, it is built up over a period of time. The ingredients that contribute to trust-building are the following:

First of all, there is the factor of competence. People in positions of leadership must not only be perceived but in actuality must be competent individuals able to distinguish primary from secondary issues. Being able to define problems clearly and face conflict is essential in a leader. Leaders must also possess expertise in one or more areas and be able to grasp the overall goals of organizations with a sense of vision. There is no substitute for competence in helping to establish trust at all levels of human endeavor.

Second, the leader must be a committed person. Commitment and competence are equally important. Both are essential to positive leadership. Commitment for Christians means a genuine allegiance to Jesus Christ and to the mission of the church, giving of one's self ungrudgingly in time, talent, and resources. Authentic commitment becomes contagious and inspires people to follow. Most of us, as I see it, are committed within limits. No one wants to be fanatical; we constantly rationalize our priorities and place limits on our commitment.

41

The ultimate test of commitment is the giving of one's life, symbolized in the cross of Christ. Most of us live within a context of reservations that we justify *ad nauseam.* Unfortunately, too many of us are like "Jonah," running from our call to commitment.

Third, leaders must have moral character. Spiritual and moral qualities gain the respect of followers. Knowing we are not perfect, we are exhorted to practice forgiveness with one another building character through prayer, discipline, and the empowerment given through the Holy Spirit.

The fourth characteristic of leadership is a caring attitude toward everyone in and out of the organization. In practice, this is almost impossible, but every effort in this direction will build trust among the membership. Perhaps no leader deserves complete trust; we are all subject to temptations and shortcomings. Nevertheless, a caring spirit must be sought toward the humblest of followers, for we are all created in God's image and have value.

Fifth, a leader must practice cooperation. Collegiality is important in effective leadership. No one is strong enough alone. We need one another and are dependent in so many ways. Collegial leadership understands the nature of ownership and is secure enough to seek the wisdom, talent, and resources of others.

Sixth, leadership requires the creative ability to see several solutions to a problem, the ability to work in more than one direction. The resolution of conflict often needs a both/and approach. Creative leadership looks beyond the dilemma, beyond the Catch-22 aspects, and finds opportunities inspired by a vision beyond the routine or restrictions of past history. Creativity underlies fruitful leadership, seeking to make new history as the winds of God's Spirit pushes us ahead.

The seventh ingredient toward developing trust in leadership is the ability to communicate. Leaders must articulate our essential mission through whatever means and media are available. Good communication depends on knowing and explaining issues with a simplicity that also accounts for the complexity involved. The ability to communicate with a sense of concreteness and understanding will engage persons in discussion and action.

Eighth, leadership also needs the courage to act. Leadership requires risk taking, the guts to take action and to look beyond endless debates.

Ninth and last, every leader brings to the arena some charm or charisma that is needed for the moment. The matching of a particular gift to a situation can make the difference in how the membership reacts. In an age of mass media and cosmetics it is difficult at times to distinguish natural charisma from hyped-up images. The leader's charisma can be that added quality of excitement needed in motivating an organization.

These then are the qualities essential for creating an atmosphere of trust in leadership—(1) competence, (2) commitment, (3) character, (4) caring, (5) cooperation, (6) creativity, (7) communication, (8) courage, and (9) charisma. Call it the "Nine C's of Leadership" necessary for maintaining credibility and confidence.

Beyond Trust, What's Needed?

While the recovery of church power calls for trust in leadership, we must not neglect the financial realities of life. *Money is also a source of power in our society.* We are not always honest in the church about money; our rhetoric often denies its importance. We learn quickly, however, that both program and prophetic witness require dollars. If all church members were tithers, we would have a powerful bargaining chip in an economically oriented society. Our giving per member in mainline churches is less than 2 percent today. This financial weakness causes us to be preoccupied with dividing scarce dollars, politicizing and emasculating our witness in society. Strong leadership plus adequate financial funds are important factors toward the recovery of church power.

In addition to trust in leadership and money, the recovery of church power calls for a rediscovery of our *vocation as God's people* through baptism. In other words, our Christian vocation is discipleship. Our avocation is how we earn our living. Unfortunately, we have twisted this around. Earning a living has become more important than witnessing. Today, we pay clergy to be "witnesses," perhaps to show the rest of us that it doesn't pay to witness. We have lost the meaning of our ordination to priesthood through baptism.

The biblical call for "the priesthood of all believers" applies to each of us without distinction. We are called upon to be chaplains to one another in the name of Christ. The People of God are "a called people" to serve and to witness, whenever and wherever we are. To recover this outlook and attitude will give us considerable momentum in recovering power as a church. For too long we have been a divided church with a minority of participants and a majority of observers. We are perceived erroneously at times as a church of clergy vs. a church of laity. Our Reformation heritage has been eclipsed. Reclaiming our vocation as the People of God will stimulate our involvement again throughout society and encourage us to work for Christian standards on behalf of everyone everywhere.

My final point in recovering church power *calls for a reaffirmation and acceptance of ourselves.* If God is so accepting of us in Christ in spite of ourselves, why aren't we a more affirming fellowship? For too long we have been negative and masochistic with ourselves. It is time to praise one another and celebrate each small victory. Pride by itself is dangerous; it can cut us off from God, but it can also restore our sense of self-esteem if the foundation of our pride is carefully rooted in God's grace. We live from grace to grace, and this fact reminds us over and over again that we came into the world naked and we will leave naked. The important question is whether we are being faithful with the stewardship of life vested in us. To this end, we must initiate an aggressive program of Christian education focused on affirmation, acceptance, and sharing for all ages, thus emphasizing a wholistic approach to discipleship.

To sum it up, our churches must have not only a strong program in evangelism, but we must also develop (1) trust in leadership, (2) adequate financial resources, (3) a renewed sense of vocation as the People of God, and (4) a renewed spirit of affirmation and acceptance in our fellowship together. When these four forces converge, we will be moving in our journey toward renewal and excellence.

Chapter 7.
Marketing the Church's Ministry

Trust in church leadership is essential to effective outreach. Communicating this quality of trust between the pulpit and pew will make churches more attractive to enquirers. This brings us next to the question of the pros and cons of marketing the church's message and ministry to society at large. What obligation do churches have to broadcast their programs to as wide an audience as possible?

Within the ranks of professional ministry, most of us do not want to admit that we are in the business of selling—whether promoting the church's program, recruiting able candidates for leadership positions, or raising the annual budget for our churches. Aren't these moments of "selling" in the church's life? Are we willing to weigh the liabilities and assets looking to Madison Avenue for assistance?

In a recent conversation with a colleague at the seminary, the relationship of marketing and ministry came up. My colleague strongly objected to the use of the word *selling.* When I probed for a reason, he responded, "Selling indicates that we have surrendered to the American business ethos. The gospel isn't a product we sell; the church commissions us to share it fully and freely with others. We are above the practice of peddling the gospel. To do so would indicate that we had succumbed to a consumer attitude toward our gospel."

I can certainly appreciate my colleague's stance, and to a large extent I agree with his sentiments. However, does that enable us to circumvent the reality that marketing—the strategy of responding and selling to real needs—is being practiced nevertheless in our churches, once we strip ourselves of pious language? Instead of using the word *selling,* we substitute other labels, such as stewardship, witness, sharing, mission, etc.

I asked an active layperson in the life of the church what she thought about the use of the term *selling.* She replied by saying, "How can we escape it?" When I mentioned that most professionals in the life of the church have negative feelings toward selling, she answered, "Visit a seminarian a month after graduation and ask the recent graduate in a new parish what they think. Most seminarians will quickly find that they are immersed in selling and promoting church programs. The reality is there; how can you avoid it?" Another layperson said to me, "I don't object to the fact of selling, per se, but it all depends on how it is done in the life of the church." One person pointed out to me that selling is an integral part of our existence. And another answered, "Of course, the biblical message is not something you buy, but there is certainly an element of communicating or marketing involved in reaching out to others." How else are others going to know we have excellent programs and services to offer?

My spotty interviews among the laity indicate that many think the church is in the selling game, whether or not the professional ministry is willing to admit it. Why do mainline clergy, with the notable exception of Robert Schuller, deny that they are in the selling business? Is it because the clergy look down upon those in the marketplace who sell for a living? Do marketing and selling smack too closely of insincerity? Do we feel ourselves compared to a used car salesperson or a television evangelist?

I have heard, as undoubtedly you have, that we are not in the selling business—the gospel of Jesus Christ is a gift of God. There are no price tags attached. We are to share the gospel with others without charge. This is sound Christian theology, but why do we spend so much money, time, and talent promoting our message? Isn't all this promoting a form of marketing and often not too sophisticated at that? Aren't we all subject to the selling mentality of our prevailing culture? Frankly, I don't think we can escape it; even if we are able to pile layers of piousness to describe our activities, we are nevertheless still selling. Why are we chagrined at times when we are labeled as "salesmen" or "saleswomen" for Jesus? Is it because we are doing a poor job of selling, or is it because we feel the sacredness of our calling has been diminished?

In one Pittsburgh Seminary program we invite distinguished laypeople to spend time in residence on campus. One of our recent guests was a business executive. This business executive explained to faculty and students why he shifted careers from being a pastor to management in industry, where for the last sixteen years he has been successfully climbing the corporate ladder. At the time of his visit with us he was vice president of his firm. The question was asked, "Why did you change from ministry to industry?" He responded by saying, "I did not find that my parish ministry was really addressing the realities of the economic-oriented society in which we find ourselves. I was not unhappy at being a pastor; I simply was not effective in ministering to the marketplace where my parishioners lived."

"In fact," he went on to say, "I unconsciously was looking down my nose at the selling world surrounding the church. Even though I was not willing to admit it consciously, in my psyche, those who were in the business of selling were second-class individuals, from my vantage point. I wanted everyone to climb up on my pedestal and view the lofty heights where I thought ministry was to take place."

Like Zacchaeus, our campus guest discovered the need to climb down from his tree and move in the midst of the world with Jesus, to rediscover the realities of the marketplace. Most clergy would rather not compare themselves to Zacchaeus; after all, Zacchaeus was a questionable tax collector, serving an unpopular government. But how different is Zacchaeus from an active pastor? As long as we are willing to receive the offerings on Sunday, sing the doxology, and pronounce the benediction, we are the Zacchaeuses of the sanctuary from the height of our pulpits, attempting to launder the taintedness of the marketplace before God. Are we really qualitatively different from Zacchaeus? Every dollar contributed is tainted, and every hand that touches that money is also within the circle of corruption and in need of redemption. Most of us understand this quite well in our reflective moments. In our psyche, however, we want to be purer than Zacchaeus, and herein lies our ministerial blindness.

Marketing or Calling?

We are all a part of a selling world; there really is no escape from this reality, no matter how much we might detest it. The Christmas and Easter seasons of buying and selling describe our culture. The church as a volunteer organization lives within this culture and is forced to sell itself to the world. We may express our selling in other terms than those practiced by the business community, but we are nevertheless selling our program. Our stewardship drives and promotional materials in the name of evangelism and Christian commitment are forms of marketing, and we are comfortable in following this format because we feel we have something vital to contribute to the community where we live and to society at large. If this is so, why shouldn't we become professional in our "marketing" endeavors? There are talented and knowledgeable people in our congregations waiting to be asked, and allies on the outside waiting to help, but afraid to volunteer since the church has indicated in so many ways that we are not in the "selling game."

I was introduced not long ago to an active churchman who owned his own public relations firm. Looking for a professional touch to our publications and brochures at the seminary, I mentioned our restricted budget (and what church organization isn't running lean these years?) and asked if he would like to contribute his time and expertise, to be a consultant for us without fee. He was surprised at first by my candor and then replied, "Why not? The most the church has ever asked me to do in the past is to be an usher. This is the first time I have been asked to do something where my talents can come into play."

This layman's comments indicate that we may not be employing effectively the lay talent before us. We tend to be too restrictive in tapping the abilities of laypeople. Often the church spends much time recruiting church school teachers, people to help in the maintenance of the plant, sing in the choir, serve on committees, donate finances, and then goes no further. *The selling talent of our laity in a selling world has not been utilized effectively, and the recent decades of decline among the mainline churches is ample evidence that we have failed to employ the diversity of talent in our midst.* Billy Graham has become over the years our "mainline" ecumenical evangelist whose voice and ways should be studied and taken seriously by church establishments, rather than ignored and criticized for the most part.

The challenge is there for us today to become a responsive and creative coalition of Christians reaching out in a more meaningful way by communicating this precious gospel of ours to a marketplace world seeking direction. Society is looking for thoughtful guidelines on how to live a worthwhile life amidst the nuances and complexities of human existence that defy pious cliches and easy panaceas.

Marketing and Mission

Our calling as Christians is clear—through baptism we have but one vocation—to live and die in Christ. Everyone is called to minister. This is what we affirm when we state in theological parlance that we believe in "the priesthood of all believers." Each of us is called upon to be a chaplain (a priest) to one another. This is our common mission. However, the mandate has somehow been lost; we have indeed become a church of clergy protective of our professional status, on the one hand, and a church of laity becoming increasingly disenchanted with the church, on the other hand. As a result, clergy and laity alike are being victimized and bombarded daily by a selling world pushing religious and nonreligious products that need to be questioned. As long as we refuse to master the selling game within our society we will be no match to the alien forces causing us to espouse a narrow and ill-defined message. Unless we learn to utilize the expertise of the laity within our churches we will not reach a larger world subjected daily to buying an inferior brand of good news. The question isn't marketing versus calling; we must see the connection between marketing and mission and thereby regain our perspective and initiative in a selling world as we market a biblical and fulfilling gospel that is neither legalistic nor simplistic.

Of course, we do not like to think of Jesus as "the salesman" who gave his life for us, but we are in agreement that his dedication for our redemption was total. He communicated this fact in an earthy way through words, deeds, and finally on the cross. Jesus was continually on the move, reaching out to his contemporaries—at Bethlehem, Nazareth, Jerusalem, and finally at Calvary. His parables were insightful eye-openers to God's kingdom of good news. He developed a network through his disciples, who in turn multiplied manyfold through the inspiration and empowerment of God's Spirit.

In the final analysis, our own organizing and marketing must also be subject to God's inspiration and empowerment. Slick marketing may be effective on the first go-around, but it will not sustain itself if God's Spirit is not present. Our marketing must be subject to God's creativity and will, as we work in a prayerful and dependent spirit. We must never allow our programs of outreach (marketing) to become ends in themselves. This would depersonalize us as it has already done to large segments of the advertising industry.

To summarize, we have not been doing a good job of marketing the church's message or services that can enhance lives and communities. We have not employed the finest professional talent available. That is to say, we have not mobilized the resources of our laity, many of whom understand better than the professional clergy that we are living in a selling world. We must master this worldly existence and advance the church's healing word of forgiveness to an audience waiting to be touched by God's solid message of hope.

Chapter 8.

What Can Churches Expect from Seminaries?

If we are to successfully integrate the practice of ministry and theological education, churches need to realistically assess what they can and cannot expect from seminaries. Do churches and seminaries have common expectations for excellence in ministry? Are we working toward the same aim? An examination of the myths and realities of theological education might be a helpful way to conclude our discussion.

"What can we expect from our seminaries?" I was asked recently. Such a direct and simple question might get an automatic reflex answer from a seminary president. However, I wanted to provide this questioner (and others) with more than a cliché in response.

Seminary Half-Truths or Myths

To begin with, several half-truths or myths currently circulating about seminaries need to be addressed. *First is the myth that seminary is where you learn the science of spirituality.* More specifically, the expectation is that one finds in seminary the knowledge and the techniques of prayer. If this were true, perhaps everyone ought to go to seminary for at least a course on prayer. It is true that clergy are expected to pray publicly, not only in worship services, but in all phases of civic religion in our society. Most ministers learn quickly that stringing words together beautifully is not necessarily prayer before God. In fact, the professionalization of prayer can become quite hollow as clergy after clergy turn prayers into lectures on God. There is no doubt that we need to be taught how to pray but not necessarily through seminary courses. We have come to realize slowly and often painfully from experience that prayer is more of an unmastered art than a science. It is more a matter of listening

51

than speaking, a letting go of formulas and allowing God to reveal the beauty of divine grace in action. Seminary education ought to intensify in us the struggle for a closer union with God.

Intellectually this calls for careful analysis of the forces that separate us from God and true prayer. The theological quest always confronts us with mystery in our search for meaning. Listening prayer teaches us to step into mystery beyond our unanswered questions. Chapel services and campus prayer rooms, as well as our discussions in and out of class, remind us that how we pray and what we pray actually reveal the quality of our relationship to God and to one another. There are neither scientific nor theological formulas of prayer that can guarantee us a successful relationship with God. It is a constant struggle of letting go and allowing God into our lives. Indeed, seminary is where we discover afresh the prayer Jesus taught his disciples.

The second myth is the expectation that seminary is a trade school to turn out preachers. The assumption here is that seminary education should consist of a series of "how-to" courses; in fact, a host of seminary critics insist that we are not practical enough in exposing seminarians to the daily realities of church life. Some even say that 90 percent of seminary education is irrelevant and so is the faculty.

In reality, seminary education is very much concerned with guiding future ministers to preach, teach, and care more effectively. Before preaching, teaching, and caring can be carried out adequately, the seminarian needs to be versed in the biblical materials and languages, develop a theological framework of thinking, and articulate the ethical norms required within a global society constantly threatening its very existence. The seminary is indeed much more than a trade school. It is the church's graduate school of leadership, preparing men and women to integrate wisely the Word of God to the human situation. As one of my colleagues indicated to me, the task of the seminary is to challenge seminarians to understand Christianity in ways that haven't been conceived before and thereby liberate themselves to think more creatively and competently on how to relate faith to complex contemporary problems.

The ministry of any seminary graduate will be measured by the level of trust earned by that graduate at the grassroots.

The graduate who effectively relates the Word of God to the local situation will be heard. We live in a suspicious society that increasingly mistrusts all professionals. The trust that ministers earn will depend on how well they integrate the information gained in school and make it applicable to people's lives. The seminary is an intellectual center that translates the gospel to the culture of the day; it is much more than a trade school of ecclesiastical technicians sent out to maintain and repair tired churches.

The third myth is the expectation that the seminary is where you find community. I suspect there isn't a seminary in the country that isn't in search of community. At an ecumenical conference for seminary presidents, every participant indicated that the seminarians on their campuses were searching for community. "Where is the seminary community I expected to find?" is the perennial question asked each year by students. Each year we must remind ourselves that the community of the seminary is an emerging reality; it is something we need to shape and build at the beginning of each new academic year. Every commencement in May marks the beginning of an emerging new community in September. The seminary community, in other words, is in a constant state of change. By its very nature it can never be static.

In a real sense, we are unable to take a photographic picture of the seminary community; it is constantly in motion, not allowing us to focus on permanence. We need to work on community together each year to make it happen. It can never be taken for granted. Each of us either contributes or inhibits community in our role as faculty, students, staff, trustees, etc. By the time the seminary pilgrimage is completed, the seminarian will have experienced community as a moving target, not something that can be isolated and dissected. The actual dynamics of community defies, I believe, intellectual analysis; it is a lived experience with opportunities each day to make or break it.

The fourth myth is the expectation that seminary is where you lose your faith. The danger is that the sacred materials will become altogether too familiar and thereby lose their sense of sacredness for us. Many seminarians will be driven sometime during their studies into serious doubts vis-à-vis the authoritative sources of their faith, while others will never quite understand why God is apparently so absent in the midst of life's tragedies. And there are some for whom the forced intellectualizing of faith makes theological knowledge seem esoteric and unrelated to life.

Quite frankly, seminary is *not* where we lose faith but where we confront the dark tunnel of despair and wonder if there is any light at the end. It is precisely at these moments that we have an opportunity for growth, as we discard vestiges of inherited faith that we have long since outgrown intellectually and persist in carrying as emotional baggage. Seminary education is an intellectual housecleaning in faith. Its aim is to nurture a firmer and more enduring setting for one's *first love*. In no way does seminary education wish to destroy that first fervor, which has been such a motivating power in one's personal pilgrimage. The sad observation is those seminarians who either haven't had a strong belief or who have guarded it so cautiously in clenched fists that all life is squeezed out.

Some students have come to my office with a concern about losing their faith, when in reality they are on the brink of shedding the old outer shell that has been restricting the growth cells within and preventing their first love to mature. As we grow out of children's clothes into a larger size, so must we allow our theological development to take place, allowing cells of living faith to multiply into an everexpanding understanding of the good news that we know in Jesus Christ. This shedding of "old skins" ought to be an endless process for faculties as well as students.

We simply cannot go on limiting our love to the backyards of our own childhood faith. The aim of seminary education is to expand our backyards, to elevate our struggles on how to live *in* but not *of* the world. Seminarians who bring a healthy and lively intellectual curiosity to seminary and are willing to take risks in widening their intellectual turf will uncover God's expanding universe of grace revealed so preeminently in Jesus Christ.

Realities of Seminary Education

Beyond these myths of seminary education, certain realities can be expected. First and foremost is the expectation that seminaries are learning centers. There is valuable information stored in the minds of our learned faculties and in excellent libraries on theological campuses, ready to be imparted to those who seek. Furthermore, the rate of academic research is constantly pushing faculties to new developments in each of their fields of study. The heart of any educational enterprise is reliable information; the seminary is no exception. Every accredited seminary community is dedicated to keeping us informed through teaching and research, comparable to reputable universities.

Second, *seminaries offer specialized opportunities for theological reflection on important issues,* such as God, life, love, and death. To wrestle with these issues is to better understand ourselves. The process of reflection is both critical and constructive. Reflection is stimulated by the information garnered from lectures, readings, and discussions. The best times for reflection follow disciplined periods spent in contemplative prayer and in informal conversations with faculty, peers, and friends. Reflection is required to nurture theological maturation.

Reflection also enables us to ask penetrating questions of ourselves. Will we contribute to the church's renewal or decline? Do our theological analyses and ethical suggestions truly comprehend the real needs of our culture? Why are we allowing the concept of the sacred to replace God, the term *relationships* to replace love, and the new science of thanatology to replace the reality of death and resurrection? What difference does an adequate Christology really make in addressing the human situation? Why is sin no longer taken seriously? Where is the power of forgiveness in our lives, and why are we such an unforgiving society? To what extent are the prophetic and pastoral dimensions of the church in opposition to each other? Allowing space for reflection enables us to ponder these and other difficult questions as we shape our foundations for ministry.

Third, *seminary education introduces us to the reality and benefits of networking among future colleagues in ministry.* Professional networking begun in seminary can provide a lifetime of support, friendships, and growth. Seminary is the place to discover our unity in diversity within the Body of Christ. Such a vision of unity will strengthen a lifelong ministry through consultations, theological challenges, and genuine friendships.

Seminarians who have experienced a mutual bonding on campus can model within their local communities the benefits of Christian community. Such an achievement will promote unity with diversity based upon trust.

Fourth, *seminary is where we fashion a realistic model for ministry.* Many options for ministry will be discussed in the course of one's seminary education, and through this means each of us can fashion a personal style of ministry to pursue.

There is much talk in seminary circles on the merits of pastoral ministry vis-à-vis specialized ministries. Seminaries provide opportunities to look at these options and offer situations to experiment with various styles of leadership practiced in ministry. We hope each seminarian will fashion a personal model that will have a positive impact on society.

The above list of myths and realities found in seminaries is by no means complete. The challenge has never been greater for theological education. Today, graduate professional schools in all fields are seeking ethical direction; church denominations need a new sense of commitment to break from fixed moorings. The entire religious enterprise, and not simply the television evangelists, must restore credibility and stability. Creative approaches must be initiated in facing global threats from nuclear holocaust; AIDS and other threats must be constructively addressed. In short, seminaries have an obligation to face these challenges and to provide competent theological education and hope that will leaven the flatness of our existence and point us toward a vision of the kingdom of God.

Postscript

We began with the question, "Where's the passion for excellence in the church?" The urgency inherent in this question has been evident throughout the chapters of this discussion. Churches and seminaries preoccupied solely with survival may not deserve to survive. Only as we look beyond survival and reach out with a passion for excellence in discipleship will we achieve a significant role in society.

One practical step toward excellence can be made through our use of time: Many of us feel victimized by the lack of time in our busy agenda, but the fact remains that each of us is either blessed or cursed with twenty-four hours each day.

The use or misuse of time significantly affects our lives, not to mention our ministries. A survey by the Association of Theological Schools indicates that the number one source of stress among seminarians is not having enough time. Unfortunately, this pressure remains throughout our lives. Failure to take charge of time can be a significant factor leading to burnout in ministry.

There are 168 hours per week. Each weekly period can be divided roughly in fourths—25 percent at work, 25 percent in sleep, 25 percent in personal maintenance and leisure, and 25 percent is "up for grabs," usually revealing the intensity of interest and priorities toward the other three categories (work, sleep, personal maintenance and leisure). Frankly, it is what we do with this last quarter, our elective time, that indicates our passion for excellence in discipleship.

What attitudes should we bring to each twenty-four hour period that is ours to spend? In the first place, we ought to lear to *enjoy* each hour. We live by grace, not by a curse. Tir is our servant, not our master. Isn't time a friend to en

rather than an enemy to conquer? It is bestowed equally by God upon us all.

Second, *evaluate* each day. Review each day in retrospect and ask what lessons have been learned or unlearned. Keeping a journal or diary is helpful in this process. Having a good friend or critic to reflect together may be beneficial for both. Without evaluation, insights are often lost and the lessons of the past day, week, month, and year are forgotten. Evaluation is essential in our pursuit of excellence.

Third, *expand* each day. Don't be satisfied with a routine schedule; maximize the gift of time that God has given. God does not expect us to be satisfied with our routine schedules but to find ways to enrich the meaning and importance of each day. In short, live each day fully to capture the driving force exemplified by the Reformers—Luther, Calvin, Knox, Wesley, and others.

Fourth, *educate* yourself each day. Spend time each day, not only in prayer and scriptural meditation (I categorize these under personal maintenance), but also use your elective time (the 25 percent that is up for grabs) to read, travel, and engage in ongoing educational opportunities. Develop an annual study plan with specific objectives. As I reflect on my seminary degree earned over thirty years ago, I know that by today's measurements it is outdated; however, it was the basis from which I could continue to grow and learn. A continuing program of disciplined self-education is the difference between a nurturing or stagnant ministry.

Recognizing the equality in time we all share, let us encourage one another to (1) enjoy each hour, (2) evaluate each day, (3) expand and enrich each week, and (4) continue to educate ourselves for fruitful years of nurturing ministry under the guidance of the Holy Spirit.

Bibliography

Armstrong, Richard S. *Pastor as Evangelist.* Philadelphia: Westminster Press, 1984.

Brown, Robert McAfee. *Spirituality and Liberation: Overcoming the Great Fallacy.* Philadelphia: Westminster Press, 1988.

Bruggemann, Walter, Sharon Parks, and Thomas H. Groome. *To Act Justly, Love Tenderly, Walk Humbly: An Agenda for Ministers.* New York: Paulist Press, 1986.

Calian, C. S. *Today's Pastor in Tomorrow's World.* Rev. ed. Philadelphia: Westminster Press, 1982.

Farley, Edward. *Theologia.* Philadelphia: Fortress Press, 1983.

———. *The Fragility of Knowledge: Theological Education in the Church and the University.* Philadelphia: Fortress Press, 1988.

Hough, Joseph C. Jr., and Cobb, John B. Jr. *Christian Identity and Theological Education.* Decatur, GA: Scholars Press, 1985.

Hudnut, Robert K. *This People, This Parish.* Grand Rapids: Zondervan, 1986.

Leith, John H. *The Reformed Imperative: What the Church Has to Say That No One Else Can Say.* Philadelphia: Westminster Press, 1988.

Lodge, George C. *The American Disease.* New York: New York University Press, 1986.

Luecke, David S. and Southard, Samuel. *Pastoral Administration: Integrating Ministry and Management in the Church.* Waco: Word Publishers, 1986.

Malony, H. Newton, Needham, Thomas L., and Southard,

Samuel. *Clergy Malpractice*. Philadelphia: Westminster Press, 1986.

Moltmann, Jürgen. *The Church in the Power of the Holy Spirit*. San Francisco: Harper & Row, 1977.

Nouwen, Henri. *Creative Ministry*. New York: Doubleday, 1971.

———. *Wounded Healer*. New York: Doubleday, 1972.

———. *Reaching Out*. New York: Doubleday, 1975.

Peters, Thomas. *Thriving on Chaos: Handbook for Management Revolution*. New York: Alfred A. Knopf, 1987.

Peters, Thomas and Waterman, Robert. *In Search of Excellence*. New York: Warner Books, 1984.

Peters, Thomas and Austin, Nancy. *A Passion for Excellence*. New York: Random House, 1985.

Schaller, Lyle. *Looking in the Mirror: Self-appraisal in the Local Church*. Nashville: Abingdon Press, 1984.

———. *The Pastor and the People*. Rev. ed. Nashville: Abingdon Press, 1986.

———. *It's A Different World!* Nashville: Abingdon Press, 1987.